DISCOVERY READERS
™

Where Did Your Family Come From?

A Book About Immigrants

by Melvin and Gilda Berger
Illustrated by Robert Quackenbush

Ideals Children's Books • Nashville, Tennessee

The authors, artist, and publisher wish to thank the following for their invaluable advice and instruction for this book:

Jane Hyman, B.S., M. Ed. (Reading), M. Ed. (Special Needs), Ed. D. (candidate)

Rose Feinberg, B.S., M. Ed. (Elementary Education), Ed. D. (Reading and Language Arts)

R.L. 2.0 Spache

Text copyright © 1993 by Melvin and Gilda Berger
Illustrations copyright © 1993 by Robert Quackenbush

Published by Ideals Publishing Corporation
Nashville, Tennessee 37214

Printed and bound in the United States of America.

Library of Congress Cataloging-in-Publication Data

Berger, Melvin.
    Where did your family come from?: a book about immigrants/by Melvin and Gilda Berger; illustrated by Robert Quackenbush.
        p.   cm.—(Discovery readers)
    Summary: Discusses immigration, past and present, focusing on how four children from different countries came to live in the United States.
    ISBN 0-8249-8647-4 (lib. bdg.)—ISBN 0-8249-8610-5 (pbk.)
    1. Immigrants—United States—Juvenile literature. 2. United States—Emigration and immigration—Juvenile literature. [1. Immigrants. 2. United States—Emigration and immigration.] I. Berger, Gilda. II. Quackenbush, Robert M., ill. III. Title. IV. Series.
JV6450.B47   1993
325.73—dc20

                               92-28626
                                    CIP
                                    AC

Discovery Readers is a registered trademark of Ideals Publishing Corporation.

Produced by Barish International, New York.

Meet Boris, Maria, Rosa, and Chang.
Each was born in a different
country.
Each came to the United States to
live.

3

Many people come to live in the
    United States.
They are called immigrants.
Any person who moves to a new
    country is an immigrant.
The United States is a land made up
    mostly of immigrants.
You and I are most likely
    immigrants too.

Either

—we came to this country

—our parents came to this
country

—our grandparents came to this
country

—someone in our family came to
this country long ago.

The first immigrants came hundreds
of years ago.

The Native Americans were here already.
They were here long before the Pilgrims.

Since then millions of immigrants have come to the United States.
Most arrived by ship.
Some of their ships sailed past the Statue of Liberty.
The Statue of Liberty is in New York harbor.
The ships landed at nearby Ellis Island
Others came by ship to California.

Today immigrants still come to the United States.

Most come in airplanes, not ships.
The airplanes land at airports
    around the country.

All immigrants want a better life.
    Some come to be free.
    Some come to be safe.
    Some come to earn more money.
    Some come to be near relatives.

Living here changes the immigrants.
They take on many American ways.
Some decide to become citizens.

To become a citizen, you must
   —be at least eighteen years old
   —be able to read and write in English
   —pass a test about American
      history and government
   —promise to obey this nation's laws
   —have   lived in this country for
      at least five years.

The immigrants also bring change
to the United States.
They bring their own special ways.

Immigrants have brought
—pizza and the waltz
—soccer and bowling
—Christmas trees and Santa Claus
—chopsticks and sushi.

Immigrants bring skills and talents.
They become
—singers and scientists
—doctors and dancers
—teachers and taxi drivers
—farmers and firefighters
—laborers and lumberjacks
—pilots and professors
—actors and artists.

How do people become immigrants?
First they must get a visa (VEE-za).
The visa allows them to enter this
    country.
It comes from the United States
    government.
To get a visa, people must be healthy.
They must be people who obey the law.
They must have a good reason for
    coming.

Once the immigrants arrive, they
    must
        —find a place to live
        —get a job or go to school
        —learn the language
        —make new friends
        —get used to American ways.

All immigrants have problems at
    first.
Immigrants past.
Immigrants present.

Now get to know Boris, Rosa, Maria,
    and Chang.
They are four new immigrants.
Find out
        —why they came
        —how they are getting along
        —what they want in the future.

∾Boris∾

Boris was born in Moscow.
Moscow is a city in Russia.

Boris's father was a top scientist.
He worked in a big lab.
The lab had very little money.
Boris's father could not do his
    experiments.

One day Boris's father got a letter.
It came from a lab in the United
   States.
The letter asked him to come to the
   United States.
There he would be able to do his
   experiments.

Boris's father really wanted to go.
He talked it over
      —with Boris's mother
      —with Boris
      —with Grandma.

Only Grandma did not want to go.
"I am too old," she said.
"But you must go.
It will be good for you."

No one wanted to leave Grandma
   behind.
But Boris's father had important
   work to do.
Sadly he asked for three visas.

Many months passed.
Finally the visas were ready.
Now Boris's family could go to the
   United States.

Soon it was time to say good-bye.

Everyone kissed and hugged
    Grandma.

Boris cried.

Maybe he would never see her again.

Then the taxi came.

It took them to the airport.

The plane left Moscow one snowy
    morning.

It landed many hours later in New
    York City.

Boris wore his heavy coat and fur hat.
He felt hot.
New York City was much warmer
    than Moscow.

The next few weeks were very busy.
Boris's family moved into an
    apartment in New York City.
They learned to ride the subways.
They shopped in a supermarket for
    the first time.

Boris started school.
But he could not read or write in
English very well.
He made many mistakes.
Some of the children laughed at
him.

Then Boris met Tommy.
Now Tommy and Boris are best
friends.
Tommy helps Boris learn English.
Boris teaches Tommy how to play
chess.

Boris is getting used to life in the
   United States.
His father is doing experiments at
   the lab.
His mother is teaching Russian.

Everyone misses Grandma.
Each week Boris sends her a letter.
His letters always end the same way:
"I wish you were here. Love, Boris."

❧Rosa❧

Rosa was born in Taxco (TAHS-ko).
Taxco is a small city in Mexico.

Rosa lived outside the city.
Her father was a farmer.
He grew corn, onions, and tomatoes.

It was a small farm.
Rosa's father had to do all the work
    by hand.
He worked very hard.
But he did not earn much money.

Rosa's house had only one room.
It had no running water or electricity.
The toilet was outside.

Rosa's mother cooked over an open
    fire.
Mostly she cooked rice and beans.
She also made tortillas
    (tor-TEE-yahs).
Tortillas are thin pancakes made out
    of cornmeal.
Mexicans eat them like bread.

Each Saturday was market day.
The whole family walked into Taxco.
They went to the town square.
Rosa's mother laid a blanket on the
    ground.
She spread out the vegetables to sell.

All day long, people walked by.
A few stopped and bought some
    vegetables.
Rosa and her sisters ran around and
    played.

Later Rosa's parents counted the
    money.
Usually it was only a few pesos.
They bought some rice and beans.

One day Rosa's father met a man.
The man told him about the United
   States.
"Farmers make more money there,"
   the man said.
"The schools are better too."

Rosa's mother got an idea.
They would sell the farm.
They would use the money to go to
    the United States.

Rosa's mother started to get ready.
She went to an office of the United
    States government.
It is called a consulate (CON-sul-it).

Rosa's mother said she wanted visas.
She filled out some papers.
Then she went home.

Many months went by.
Finally Rosa's mother could pick
   up the visas.
The family could go.

Rosa's parents sold the farm.
They packed up their things.
Everyone got on a bus.

The bus ride lasted for a
    day and a night.
Finally the bus stopped at a bridge.
On the other side was the
    United States.

An immigration officer met them.
She asked to see the family's visas.
Rosa's family could enter the
    United States.

The bus crossed over the bridge.
It stopped at a small town in Texas.
Other immigrants from Mexico
    lived there.
A farmer was looking for helpers.
Someone took Rosa's father to meet
    the farmer.

Rosa's father got a job.
Now he farms the land. He uses a
    tractor and other machines.
He grows some of the best
    vegetables in Texas.
The vegetables feed many people.

The farm work is very hard.
But Rosa's father earns more money than before.
The family has a better life.

Now the toilet is inside the house.
Rosa's mother cooks on a stove.
Beans, rice, and tortillas are still the main foods.
But they also eat chicken or other meat.

Now Rosa and her sisters go to school.
Rosa wants to be a teacher.
She wants to help children read and write.

꧁Maria꧂

Maria was born in Rome.
Rome is a city in Italy.

Maria's parents worked in a pizzeria
(peet-saa-REE-uh).
Maria's mother, Angela, was the
cook.
Maria's father, Antonio, was the
waiter.

Maria's Uncle Luigi (Loo-EE-gee) is
   Antonio's brother.
He moved to the United States
   many years ago.
His home is in Chicago.

Antonio and Luigi sent letters back
   and forth.
They talked on the telephone.
Each had the same wish.
It was to be together again.

Then Luigi decided to open a
   pizzeria.
He needed a cook and a waiter.
"Angela makes the best pizza," he
   said. "And Antonio always makes
   the customers happy."

Uncle Luigi wrote to Maria's
   parents.
"Come to Chicago," he said.
   "Angela will cook in my pizzeria.
   Antonio will be the waiter."

"Let's try it," said Maria's mother.
She asked for visas.
A letter came back.
"Wait for two years," it said.

Next Uncle Luigi wrote to the
   immigration office.
"Antonio is my brother," he wrote.
   "I need him and his wife to work
   in my pizzeria."
Soon three visas were ready for
   Maria's family.

Maria's family went to the airport.
They had five bags of clothes and
   other things.

Only one bag did not go with the rest.
Maria's father carried it.
The bag held his accordion.

Soon the plane took off.
Maria fell asleep.
She slept for many hours.
When she woke up, she was in Chicago.

The airport was crowded.
Maria and her family waited in a
    long line.
Everyone was from somewhere else.
Poland. Ireland. Germany.
A few were from Italy.

The immigration officer asked to
   see their visas.
"Welcome to the United States," he
   said.

Uncle Luigi was waiting at the gate.
The brothers hugged and kissed.
They put the bags into Luigi's car.
Then they drove home.

A few days passed.

Maria's parents started to work.

Now Angela makes the pizzas.

People say they are the best in
    Chicago.

Antonio waits on the tables.

Everyone loves his jokes.

Maria has many friends.

She tries to speak as they do.

She wears her hair as they do.

She dresses as they do.

Sometimes Maria gets upset.
She tells her parents she is ashamed
   of them.
They do not speak English very well.
They look old-fashioned.

Maria's father laughs.
He knows just what to do.
He takes out his accordion.
He sings some old Italian songs.

The songs make Maria feel good.
They remind her of Italy.
She loves the United States.
But she hopes always to remember
   Italy.

✵Chang✵

Chang was born in Sinpo.
Sinpo is a town in Korea.

Chang's father owned a shoe factory.
The family had lots of money.
They lived in a big house.

Then a new government took over.
They passed new laws.
One law said people could not own
    factories.

Another law was even worse.
It said factory owners would go to
    jail.

Chang's father got scared.
He decided to take his family out of
    Korea.
Late one night, they left.

The family drove to the docks.
There they found a ship.
It was old and rusty.
But it was about to sail to the
    United States.

Chang's father spoke to the ship's
    owner.
He gave him lots of money.
The family got on board.

It took the ship a long time to cross
   the ocean.
Finally it arrived in San Francisco.
Chang's family got off.

The immigration officer asked for
   visas.
"We have none," Chang's father said.
"Why did you come to the United
   States?" the officer asked.
"There is a new government in
   Korea," Chang's father said.
   "I might be thrown in jail."

The immigration officer said, "You
    are refugees.
Refugees flee a bad government.
Refugees don't need visas.
You can come into the United
    States."

Many Korean immigrants live in
    San Francisco.
One was a friend of Chang's father.
Chang's father went to look for him.

At last Chang's father found his
 friend.
He owned a grocery store.
He gave Chang's father a job.
Chang's mother also went to work
 there.

Chang's parents worked long hours.
They opened the store at dawn.
They closed it late at night.
They even worked on Saturdays and
 Sundays.

Chang's mother saved the money.
After a while, they had enough.
Chang's father opened his own
  grocery store.

The grocery sold only Korean foods.
Gingerroot. Bamboo shoots.
Korean lettuce. Leafy cabbage.
Bean sprouts. Water chestnuts.

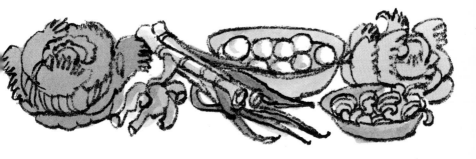

Now the whole family works in the
  grocery.
Chang's father serves the customers.
His mother tells people how to cook
  Korean foods.
Chang and his brothers keep the
  store clean.

Chang's family is always busy.
Yet sometimes they have a party.
They invite their friends.

Chang's mother wears a brightly
colored dress.
The dress was made in Korea.
She cooks Korean dishes.
After dinner they all sing Korean
songs.

Chang studies hard.
He's not sure what he wants to be.
A scientist?
A doctor?
Or maybe a businessperson like his
    father?

The choice is Chang's.
He just wants to grow up free and
    safe.

Boris. Maria. Rosa. Chang.
They are today's immigrants.
They remember their pasts.

They are part of the present.
The future belongs to them and
to us.

Index